Craig Gross &
Mike Foster

QUESTIONS YOU
can't ask your
Mama About SEX

Is it wrong to

What does God
think about
Stars?

invert

QUESTIONS YOU
can't ask your
Mama About SEX

by
Craig Gross &
Mike Foster

ZONDERVAN™

GRAND RAPIDS, MICHIGAN 49530 USA

www.invertbooks.com

Editorial direction by Doug Davidson
Art direction by Jay Howver
Proofread by Laura Gross and Janie Wilkersen
Cover design by Burnkit
Interior design by Holly Sharp

Printed in the United States

05 06 07 08 09 10 / DCI / 9 8 7 6 5 4 3 2

Acknowledgements

To our wives, Jennifer and Jeanette: Thanks for standing with us in this ministry and for giving us your loving support.

This book and this ministry would not have been possible without the help of many other people—from those who showed us how to use spell-check to those who answered our questions. More specifically, thanks to Jason Harper, Kevin and Lilly Troyer, Troy Busher, Jud Wilhite, Chris Ferebee, Wes and Ellie Beavis, Molly Kline, and Jay Howver.

And finally, to you, the writers and creators of all these questions— thanks for taking the time to seek out answers to the questions you have always wanted to ask someone.

Table of Contents

Introduction
Breaking the Silence

Sex. The very mention of the word in Christian circles causes ears to balloon like satellite dishes. Announce that this week's sermon will address a sexual topic and a pastor can be sure the pews will be filled Sunday morning. Yet there are very few, if any, churches who are willing to deal with sexuality beyond the typical youth pastor's urging young people to "save it for marriage."

Trust us, we know. Before we founded XXXchurch, each of us worked in local youth ministries. We knew our youth were struggling with everything from dating purity to Internet porn. Yet we had no idea how to address these issues without offending someone or having some naïve parent jump all over us because they desperately believed their daughter or son was immune to such "filth." Sex issues for teenagers have become the dirty little secret that nobody wants to talk about.

The results of the church's silence are astounding. You can look around any high school or shopping mall and see the results of the sexual revolution. Scantily dressed young people flaunt their bodies, advertising that they are "available." And most of the time, it's not on purpose. It is the result of confusion. Entertainment and pop culture have exposed them to too much, too soon, for too long.

Teenagers have many questions about sex, and they often have no idea where to turn for answers. Those who are already in sexually difficult places don't know where to get help or how to find freedom. Teenage pregnancies, porn, and promiscuity have produced pain in the lives of many teenagers. Fast forward a few years and these same young people can find it nearly impossible to establish a healthy long-term relationship.

Today, one out of every two marriages ends in divorce. According to Janet E. Smith, author of The Christian View of Sex:

A Time for Apologetics, Not Apologies, six out of ten teenagers are sexually active. She writes:

> The millions of abortions over the last decade and the phenomenal spread of AIDS indicate that our society has serious problems with sexuality. In the last generation, the incidence of sexual activity outside of marriage—with all of its attendant problems—has doubled and tripled—or worse. We have no particular reason to believe we have seen the peak of the growth in sex-related problems.

When we founded XXXchurch several years ago, our goal was to create a place of honest dialogue and support for Christians who struggle with issues related to pornography and sexual addiction. We wanted to offer help to Christians and non-Christians in an area of sexuality where the church has long been silent. But as the outreach has developed, we have received hundreds of questions not only about porn, but also about virtually every possible issue related to sexuality. And many of these came from teenagers who are desperate to find anyone who will give them straightforward answers to their questions about sex.

This book is our attempt to compile some of the questions and answers that are most relevant to youth who are seeking to live out their Christian faith. Since our Web site and ministry has focused a great deal on pornography and sexual addictions, you'll find those topics covered here. But this is not a book focused on porn. It's an attempt to stand with young people in their struggle for wholeness and sexual purity and to give them frank, Christian answers to the very real questions they are asking about sexuality and their faith.

We understand it can be incredibly embarrassing for teenagers to ask questions about sex. Often they are made to feel that if they do ask a question, they may be judged for its content. And all the pressure surrounding sex doesn't make talking about it any easier; it only brings a distorted attitude toward sexuality.

This is our attempt to help churches address the issue by addressing it for them. The book is a collaborative project, but most of the questions were originally answered by one of us. Since we think that personal connection is important, we tried to maintain the conversational tone in this book.

We hope young people will find this to be a valuable book that gives them answers to the questions they may be too afraid to ask and encourages them to accept God's invitation to a pure lifestyle that is completely devoted to him.

Craig Gross and Mike Foster

Chapter 1

Sex And You

Freedom, frustration, and foreplay

How far is "too far" sexually when you are not married?

Well, this is the big question for many young people, so it's probably a good starting point. The simple fact is that God does not map out word for word in the Bible what is and is not okay. It sure would be nice if he did.

But the Bible does give us a lot of guidance regarding the age-old question of "How far is too far?" Repeatedly the Bible says not to be sexually immoral. The Bible does not say just to avoid the act of sexual intercourse outside of marriage, but to avoid sexual immorality. In other words, God wants us to be sexually pure.

17

So sex is more than just intercourse?

The definition of sex needs to be widened to consider more than just intercourse. There are many sexual acts that are not intercourse. Is the action done to cause arousal? If so, it's sexual.

It is hard to be sexually pure in mind and body if you are constantly pushing the limits of what is, or is not, okay. When you push the physical or sexual boundaries when you're dating, it can be like a drug. What was exciting at first starts to seem less exciting—so you move on to the next level because you want to feel the next "high."

Why is reserving sex for marriage so important?

Sexual intimacy binds people together physically, emotionally, and spiritually. Each of these three elements is distinct from the others, yet they are dependent on one another at the same time. Sex is a beautiful mystery and a blessing when it is handled appropriately, and it is completely destructive when it is not.

Sex is the most physically intimate action you can participate in with another person. And the steps leading up to intercourse—from holding hands, to hugging and kissing, to touching another person's naked body—are all part of it. The level of intimacy that takes place in all physical actions leading up to and including sex binds those two people together physically, emotionally, and spiritually. The physical is only a representation of what is really going on inside both people emotionally and spiritually. When two people end a relationship that has gone far physically, it rips them apart, because they have made themselves so vulnerable to each other on every level.

I love my boyfriend, and he says he loves me. He tells me he wants to go a little further. How do I decide what is okay?

First, I do not question your ability to be in love. Many people fall in love as teenagers, marry their high school sweethearts, and stay married for over 50 years. And within marriage, their sexual activity is blessed as a symbol of their union.

I don't want to fall into the trap of trying to tell you exactly how far your actions should go. Instead, I would remind you that God asks that you honor him in everything you do. Many students date and display affection in ways that bring honor to God. However, they've usually set strict boundaries regarding where not to go.

These boundaries need to be established together—thinking not only of what you can handle but also of each other. If holding his hand causes him to fantasize into the land of arousal, then stop holding his hand. If his giving you a back rub gets your hormones rushing, then don't let him do it. Your lines should entrench you into staying on the purity side of things.

Once the ball of physical activity starts to roll, it can be nearly impossible to change direction. And once you have gone to a certain level of sexual intimacy, both of you will more easily go back to that level the next time.

19

I have two friends who recently got married. Both were in their mid-twenties and had dated many people before they dated each other. Each of them was so in love with who God had made the other one to be that they decided not to kiss. After dating for over a year, they were married. When they kissed on their wedding day, it was the first time they had ever kissed. That is truly a love story. Today, they are very happy and learning to explore each other's bodies as any married couple would do.

So what do you do when you're "turned on" and in love but not married yet?

Try playing a great board game like Scrabble. This will take your mind off those thoughts—or at least you'll spell some pretty outrageous words! But I guess spelling is a lot safer than what you had in mind!

On a more serious note, rethink your alone time with your boyfriend or girlfriend. It is easy to fall into temptation since you are in love. It's tough to find a couple who can honestly say they are not tempted to experiment, so why put yourself in that situation? You need to place some strict parameters around the relationship. Establish these parameters at a time when the mood is spiritual, not sexual.

One idea could be to establish ending times for dates. When you just hang out till the wee hours of the morning—and no one else is up but the two of you—you have walked onto the front lines of failure.

You could also consider going on group dates. Lots of people make for lots of fun. The pressure for intimate action is limited because of the size of the crowd.

You could also get an accountability partner, maybe an older married couple who can help you and your boyfriend or girlfriend to be accountable and sexually pure before you are ready to get married. (For more on this, see chapter 7 about accountability.)

My boyfriend and I got close, but he never actually went in me. I am still considered pure and a virgin, right?

This question is asked of us often: *Am I still a virgin?* Technically speaking, the word *virgin* is defined as one who has not had genital sex. However, the bigger issue is purity.

When you ask if you are "still pure and a virgin," you are really asking two different questions. Once mistakes have been made, purity is lost. However, we must realize that with God's help, purity can always be restored. Always. Too many people get bound by their past mistakes and give up on the pursuit of purity.

Regarding your statement, "he never actually went in me," I am concerned about how you got that far along. When two people plow through that many physical boundaries, they are nearing the point of no return. This is a place that must be avoided—not because of rules or regulations, but because you are committed to the best plan that God has established for you. That plan is one mate for life. And that can be defined only within the commitment of a marriage.

Set parameters with your boyfriend before you get caught up in the heat of the moment. This will prevent anger, frustration, and a strained relationship if you miss the mark.

My girlfriend and I are trying not to have sex before marriage, even though her mom said it was okay. So to honor our commitment we just help each other masturbate. It feels comfortable, so what is wrong?

There is more than one thing wrong with this. But let's address what is right first. Your commitment to abstain from sexual intercourse is admirable.

Now, let's consider her mom's permission. I believe honoring mom and dad is crucial. However, when our parents tell us something, we still need to be sure it aligns with God. If it doesn't, we can't use "parental permission" as a license to sin.

At this point in your life, you and your girlfriend are accountable for your own actions. Adjusting to another area of lust and sexual sin instead of having sexual intercourse should not ease your conscience. Look at what 1 Corinthians 6:9-10 (The Message) says:

> Don't you realize that this is not the way to live? Unjust people who don't care about God will not be joining in his kingdom. Those who use and abuse each other, use and abuse sex, use and abuse the earth and everything in it, don't qualify as citizens in God's kingdom. A number of you know from experience what I'm talking about, for not so long ago you were on that list. Since then, you've been cleaned up and given a fresh start by Jesus.

To think that mutual masturbation is a form of honoring your vow to purity is total deception. Keep your eyes on the goal. You and your girlfriend should stimulate each other's spiritual growth. Seek to arouse in each other a hunger to learn more about Jesus. When this happens, you truly will be worthy of dating each other.

One final question—The Bible instructs and warns us that if you cause another to fall, you will be judged. Is it possible that if you allow sexual actions into your relationship that you are causing your girlfriend to fall? If so, what makes you exempt from God's hand? It's worth thinking about.

My boyfriend and I have dry sex all the time (with clothes on) and I am the only one who has an orgasm. We don't have sex, and we both don't always orgasm at the same time—it's just pleasure, right?

Dry sex, hmmm?

What happens at the peak of compromise is really irrelevant. We hear this kind of thing a lot. For instance, some people want to say that if only one of the two people is having pleasure, then it's not a bad thing or it's not wrong. I call this Misdirected Morality. Misdirected Morality says, "If I can pleasure this other person by doing this but *I'm* not receiving pleasure, then I'm okay."

But let's break this scene down a little further. You and your boyfriend are fully clothed. Yet you are rolling around, body to body, on the floor. You are simulating the full act of sexual intercourse, yet the only thing he is penetrating is his polyester pants. Both of you are attaching your conscience, your emotions, and your affection to each other. The fact that there is still a sixteenth of an inch of clothing between you does not make this a God-blessed act.

I fear you underestimate the soul connection that is happening here. That thin layer of clothing does not have the ability to protect the purity of your hearts. It may prevent a pregnancy, but it will still leave you empty when the two of you move on to other relationships.

Some folks will argue with me about this. They will say that what you are doing is harmless. Yet I don't believe that a sexual act is okay just because it can't get you pregnant. That kind of thinking explains why so many young girls, as young as early middle school, are having dry sex and experimenting with oral sex. Many of us in youth ministries were alarmed to hear that many local middle school students were attending oral sex parties. When confronted by the school officials, the young girls had a response similar to yours. They said, "We did not have sex!" As if that would console their parents. It's Misdirected Morality.

Allow God's Word to guide you. Consider this passage from 1 Thessalonians 4:3-4 *(The Message)*: "God wants you to live a pure life. Keep yourselves from sexual promiscuity. Learn to appreciate and give dignity to your body."

24

Am I still a virgin if I've given my boyfriend oral sex?

Many hours of counseling have been spent talking with people who feel they have lost their virginity because of oral sex. The definition of a *virgin* is one who has not had sexual intercourse. Technically, people can be virgins and still engage in very sexual behaviors. So yes, you are still a virgin. But as we've said earlier, God's goal exceeds virginity. His goal is purity. And one cannot participate in oral sex outside of marriage and still be pure.

But I would caution you to guard against the trap of condemnation. Even if you have missed the mark on purity, ask God to cleanse you and then embrace the fact that you are forgiven! With his grace and strength, you'll remain on the right track.

My best friend always makes out with all her girl friends—I think she's just trying to get attention. Recently, she tried to make out with me and everyone knows. Now people are making fun of me. What should I do?

First things first—let's define what it means to be a friend. If your "best" friend is acting this way, you may need to reconsider the foundation of your friendship. A friend is a faithful listener, not a flirty luster. A friend sharpens, but doesn't seduce. A friend gives attention and doesn't always seek to get attention.

Having said that, let's take a deeper look. You stated that everyone knows and people are making fun of you. I assume they are making fun of the fact that she hit on you, not that you refused. Again, if they are making fun of you for refusing, then you need to cut these friends loose. It will be better to find some new friends—or even to be lonely—than to have to fight these battles with those who are closest to you.

Proverbs 17:9 says, "He who covers over an offense promotes love, but whoever repeats the matter separates close friends." If your friends keep talking about you and making fun of you, they should know that ultimately they will lose you.

If I have oral sex with my boyfriend and then he finishes by masturbating, would that mean I had sex with him? I didn't finish him off, and I got no pleasure for myself.

Yes, you had oral sex with him. Never has sex been qualified by whether you were in contact or initiated contact prior to, during, or after ejaculation. The fact that you are trying to fly under the purity radar is a concern. By the time you are at that point, you may have been more intimate than you can even fathom.

Oral sex is one of the most intimate acts that can occur between two people. Young people dodging the meaning of sex have lost the concept of what it means to be pure. It reminds me of a former president who did not feel he was unfaithful to his wife because of your exact scenario. In fact, many of the youth that I counsel use that very example to argue with me.

The greater picture is purity of the mind, heart, and spirit. God does not delight in the fact that you didn't finish what you started. God detests the fact that you were in that position at all. What was meant for intimacy between two married people has been diminished to a backseat romp where you "got no pleasure for yourself."

26

I want to challenge you to reaffirm your commitment to God, your future spouse, and your own purity. Use the Bible as your guideline. And don't allow yourself to be used to "start him off." You are a beloved child of God, not just a tool or a physical playground for someone else's pleasure.

All my life I have been attracted to guys as much as girls. Does this mean I am a homosexual?

Thank you for the honest question and for having the right heart to address this issue. I can tell you firmly the answer is: NO, you are not a homosexual. *Homosexual* is a term the world has dubbed for those who attach themselves sexually to a person of the same gender.

I would ask you to consider what you mean when you say you are "attracted to guys as much as girls." Recognizing that a person of the same sex is attractive hardly makes you gay. I expect you mean that you are sexually aroused by the appearance of guys.

In Genesis, we read how God created man in his image. God is perfect and just, and he created you the way you are. He designed you as a man. I believe your attraction to the same sex is due to a learned behavior. Consider this quote from an article by Bill Shepson in the July 2001 issue of Charisma:

> "I believe sexual orientation is a learned behavior and can be unlearned," says Grahame Hazell, president of Exodus in Europe, Africa, and the Middle East. "Is it easy? No. Will it always be a struggle? Usually, yes. We will always be drawn to our roots and will never be perfect this side of the cross. But God's Word says that if we align our will with his, we will make progress."

If you are struggling in this direction, what should you do?

1. Tell someone you trust. Talk to a trusted pastor, parent, or friend. Explain that the need for help is beyond your own strength.

2. Extinguish any and all behavior that is attached to the struggle. Just as we would say to any person struggling with sexual sin—remove the risk of falling into temptation. God always provides a "trapdoor" to escape.

3. Talk to an expert. Exodus International, the ministry quoted above, has a list of resources that range from Bible studies to a Live-In program that will help bring positive change.

Many of the guys and girls at my school go to "rainbow parties." I am so naïve. What are they?

As harmless as it might sound, "rainbow parties" (or "going rainbowing") are anything but harmless. It's a recent thing that has become tragically popular on both coasts.

Rainbowing is the term that describes the act of a male having multiple oral sex engagements in a row. The girls who perform the oral sex use a different color lipstick and leave their mark. At the end of the party, the guy has been "rainbowed." Often times the students are given a bracelet when they arrive at the party and they must find the girl who has the same colored bracelet.

This is absolute hedonism—and I cringe that I even have to write about this. We are moving toward a time when oral sex is becoming socially accepted because of the previous notion that it is not sex.

I pause for a moment as a father. I wonder what must have gone so tragically wrong in a girl's life for her to agree to be used in such a demoralizing way. Yet as shocking as it may seem, girls are often the ones who are throwing these parties.

To all students who are reading this—please consider this verse from 1 Corinthians 6:18 (*NKJV*): "Flee sexual immorality. Every sin that a man does is outside the body, but he who commits sexual immorality sins against his own body."

I've participated in a threesome with my boyfriend and a friend who is bisexual. I want to marry my boyfriend but still fantasize about my friend. Does that make me bisexual?

You are not bisexual. *Bisexual* is a term the world uses to describe people who act sexually impulsive with both sexes. Granted, having a threesome put you way off the path of God's best. During that time, you opened yourself up to areas and impulses you were never created to experience, and seeds of thought were planted and took root in your mind. This is why Paul the apostle said, "Take captive every thought." He is saying don't fantasize about things that will corrupt you. Now that those seeds have been planted in your mind, ask God to flush those ideas from your head.

There are three ways we suggest you do this. First, input good to overtake the bad. Exchange the impure fantasies with new thoughts from God's Word. I suggest you get into a woman's devotional that directs you to Scripture dealing with regaining sexual purity.

29

Secondly, in your times of worship and prayer, find the strength to apologize to your friend and make things right. You can communicate to her that what you did was wrong and that is not who you are. Let her know you are committed 100 percent to a heterosexual and healthy future with your spouse.

Finally, you and the man you want to marry need some premarital counseling. The fact that he was willing and actively participated does not describe the actions of the head of a home. God asks the male to be a priestly leader—to set up your home for spiritual, physical, and emotional leadership. Your boyfriend failed in all three areas. The failure can be overcome; the question is: Does he realize he missed the mark? Hold off on the marriage until you have addressed these issues of broken trust and forgiveness.

Chapter Two

Sexual Purity

No, it's not an oxymoron

My boyfriend knows about my commitment to abstain from sex until marriage, but he has promised me that we will be married. How can I keep from having sex when I really want to and everywhere I look people are doing it?

Really wanting to have sex and really wanting to please God can be a tough fight. Don't mistake the heart of God. He created sex and instructs married people to have sex and enjoy it. Yet sex can't be fully embraced or fully enjoyed unless it is in the right relationship and season.

If you are nearing the marriage date, your wanting to experience sex is understandable. Yet so many people get impatient and have sexual intercourse before marriage. It can happen out of curiosity, desire for emotional comfort, or flat-out selfishness.

33

I would ask that you make your future the higher priority. The pain and baggage of premarital sex can never be physically amended. It can often lead to an unplanned child. Then the couple may be tempted to put the wedding plans in fast-forward to make it appear as though the conception occurred during the honeymoon, and on and on and on. The entire marriage can end up being just a messed up cover-up where the couple realizes they weren't ready. Sounds great, doesn't it? God says to wait. He wants things to unfold on his timeline.

Consider why you want so badly to have sex. Many people—and this seems especially true of women—seek sex as a way to fill an emotional void or to gain affection. Others substitute it as a way to feel loved. It can never fully provide either. Trust God's wisdom and follow his lead. God's plans, timing, and perfection can't fail.

I have failed in keeping my virginity and have had sex multiple times in order for someone to love me. Am I failing because of an issue I can't see?

There are many possible issues. Getting through adolescence can be a difficult thing. But most teenagers don't have the insight that you do. You said you were having sex "in order for someone to love me." From my perspective, sex is something that occurs *because* of love, not something that *creates* love. And that love is fully illustrated when two people come together in marriage.

God defines the prerequisite for sex as marriage. Marriage sets the table by uniting two hearts, minds, and souls, not just two bodies. And having sex can create new life. God wants to assure that if a life is created, then the mother and father are in a committed relationship and prepared to raise the child together.

I encourage you to look to the Bible's words as a healthy guideline for establishing the right steps for sexual purity and relational success. Even though you have failed, God is ready to forgive you whenever you ask him to do so.

All of my life people have told me I should stay a virgin until I get married. I've been with my boyfriend for about three months, and when we are together he makes me feel so special. He wants to go further and sometimes I get lost in the moment and go there with him. How do I stop my feelings from allowing me to go too far?

Psalm 86:11 says, "Teach me your way, O Lord, and I will walk in your truth." Not only have you heard from a lot of people that

34

you should be a virgin, but you've also heard this from God. This is his commandment. This is his way.

I understand that your boyfriend makes you feel special. That is a good thing. But the payoff for feeling special cannot be to give up that feeling.

When you start to "get lost" in the moment, you need to have a standard that is based in fact, not your feelings. And the fact is God's Word. Make a healthy start a priority. Enlist the help of your boyfriend. Explain that he makes you feel special, but that this special feeling is stolen and replaced with a sleazy feeling when you have sex. Ask him how he wants you to feel—special or sleazy? It sounds like he is a great guy and will want you feel special.

35

Lastly, consider the priority of your future. Think about tomorrow, not just the feelings of today. Your future can be delayed, detoured, even destroyed if the wrong decisions are made. Choose purity.

How do I forgive myself for continually having sex when I know it's not okay?

Let the Bible bring comfort to your heart after missing the mark. Read these words from Hebrews 10:22 (*NASB*): "Let us draw near with a sincere heart in full assurance of faith, having our hearts sprinkled clean from an evil conscience and our bodies washed with pure water." The good news is that your heart has been "sprinkled clean." As a Christian, you have been forgiven by God. It is quite assuming for any of us to think we can't forgive ourselves.

This is not to say our actions are never regrettable. Of course they are. But regardless of how regrettable, there is nothing in our sexual past that is unforgivable. *Nothing*!

The key word in your question is "continuously." I would ask you to think about how you keep going back to the same area of sexual weakness. I don't mean this in a cynical, judging way. I mean how does it happen? Do you find yourself with a boyfriend who is pushy? Are you in the wrong frame of mind?

36

Let me give you an example. My wife and I once counseled a young lady who had been involved in a lot of sexual activity. She said her failures often occurred at times when she got drunk. The "how" of her situation was connected to her drinking alcohol. Rather than facing the sex issue first, I asked her to eliminate drinking to see if that helped (in more ways than one). She committed to try it. Guess what happened? Not only did she discover that she could survive socially without being drunk, but she also quit having sex. She discovered that she really didn't want to have sex, but alcohol had become her excuse to let her guard down. And having sex was just a part of her wanting to be accepted. But when a person discovers some of the plans that God has for them, the world's offers look very weak.

So I'd encourage you to look at the circumstances that cause you to do what you've said you want to avoid. And then stay out of those situations.

A final Scripture to hold you on track is 1 John 1:9: "If we confess our sins, he is faithful and just and will forgive us our sins and purify us from all unrighteousness."

I have made the commitment over and over to stay away from sex. But again and again I end up back in the bedroom with my boyfriend. I don't know what to do. Although I don't want to have sex, I can't stop in the moment. Should I even try to stay away from him?

I appreciate the fact that you keep making a commitment. We recognize that you desire to do what is right. However, the issue is maintaining the commitment and holding true to what God has asked of you. God asks you to remain pure so that you can receive all that he has for you. And he does not ask you to do anything that he will not also give you the strength to do.

There are often underlying issues for girls who continue to have sex when they don't want to. I don't buy into the idea that some girls are just "horny chicks." For the most part, a woman's emotional chemistry is not centered on physical touch. Her primary focus tends to be on making an emotional connection. When women seek physical acts as a way of primary gratification, something is usually off.

In some situations, there may be an unhealthy desire for male affection that needs to be addressed. Some girls never received enough affection or affirmation from their fathers. Because of this, they may become promiscuous to satisfy their longing for approval.

Second, there are often self-esteem issues. Gaining esteem through ways that God advised against can cost a lot of emotional, social, physical, and financial pain.

Consider the story of David and Bathsheba. King David needed the affirmation that came from the arousal of Bathsheba.

After their illicit affair, Bathsheba became pregnant with David's child. Both were already married, so they began to lie and conspired to cover up their sexual sin. Murder, deception, and ultimately the lost life of their baby were all part of the price David paid because he wanted Bathsheba's affection. He needed her to affirm him. Psalm 51 is the prayer of forgiveness that David wrote after collapsing from all the guilt. It surely was an expensive affair.

Having said all of that, don't wait until the heat of the moment to stop. Keep yourself in healthy environments where sex can't happen. If you guys can't keep your clothes on, eliminate alone time. Date with a group of friends and stay in public places where others can hold you accountable. Tell a close friend your dilemma and give a few people permission to daily ask you some accountability questions, like, "Are you honoring God's plan for your life?"

My girlfriend and I keep having sex. We can't seem to stop. What can we do?

Try spending an afternoon at your local county health office. First, the two of you can get yourselves tested to see if either of you have contracted any STDs. If you are lucky enough to have avoided infection so far, you can watch people go in and out of the office—some with smiles because they get to go back to their sin; but some with tears because now they are infected.

If you really want to keep sinning, then keep at it. But if you want help, it's all about accountability.

If your parents are Christians, tell them—you and your girlfriend *together*. Face up to your parents and deal with the consequences, however extreme they may be. Next, tell your pastor and begin going through counseling. By talking through this problem, it is necessary to identify the sources of the problem. For example, if you find that sex keeps happening in certain places at certain times, then ask others to support you in avoiding those situations.

You need to have the desire to stop. You can do anything you set your mind to do, especially if it is God's will. Trust me, it is *not* his will that you are engaging in sexual promiscuity. There are so many Scripture passages that demand purity. So act on the love you have for God. If you love God, you will keep his instructions. That's straight truth from the Bible.

39

My boyfriend and I are both Christians, and so are our families. We were home alone at his house and went too far. We had sex in his bed, and then his mom walked in on us. I've asked for forgiveness but still have not received it. What do I do?

The first priority is to make things right with God. You have done that by asking for forgiveness. But you need to make sure that your request for forgiveness includes repentance. The best definition of repentance is to turn and go in the opposite direction. Don't just say, "God, I am sorry." Say, "God, I will go in the other direction."

Second, make things right with the families—yours and his. I can't imagine how embarrassed you must have been, but still you have to make it right with the families. His mother and father are the spiritual authorities in his life and they have been offended by the behavior. Don't try to cover it up. Don't try to hide it. Own the mistake and take responsibility.

I suggest that you and your boyfriend, along with both sets of parents, sit down together, take a couple of deep breaths, and set some healthy parameters for your future. It may take some time to restore trust on all levels. But remember, it can be done.

I am 14 years old. Ever since I can remember, my mom has told me to stay pure until I am married. My parents are divorced, and she has been with different guys. Why should I listen to her? I want to do it just to make her mad. How do I tell her that she is wrong?

40

I am sorry that you are living in what appears to be a very hypocritical situation. However, in defense of your mom, you need to be sure that she is acting wrong before you confront her. The Bible says we are to honor our parents. Make sure that you honor her. It is possible to honor her and still confront her easy ways. I suggest that you explain that you know it is hard without your dad, but that she should strive to be sexually honorable, just as she's encouraged you to do.

One of the guys in my youth group once faced a very similar situation, except it involved his father. The son confronted the dad, and the dad admitted to his failures. Dad then asked for forgiveness, and the two of them set up an accountability system. Son held dad accountable, and dad did the same for his son. The conclusion to the story was that, years later, the son asked his dad to be the best man at his wedding.

Chapter Three

Pornography and the Internet

The high-tech porno pipeline

You guys have built your ministry around helping Christians with pornography. It's not really that big a problem for Christians, is it?

Porn is an incredibly difficult subject to talk about. It's seedy. The word conjures up thoughts of back alley activity. It brings to mind the old stag films that fraternities introduced to college freshmen in the '50s, or what men watch at a friend's bachelor party. The very sound of the word is edgy—PORN. Its edge is probably its greatest attribute because it makes for an awkward conversation. Add to this the fact that the church usually avoids the pronouncement of the word at all costs, and the ingredients for the "dirty little secret" incubate.

43

Yet the problem continues to spread throughout society and the church in sweeping proportions. Take a look at some of the statistics:

- 37 percent of pastors say online porn is a struggle for them.

- 720 million porn movies are watched every year.

- 77 percent of online visitors to porn Web sites are male.

- Average career length of a porn actress is one year.

- Average pay a girl receives for appearing in a porn film is $1,000.

- 72 percent of the people surveyed view porn to masturbate.

- 30 percent of all unsolicited e-mails contain pornographic material.

- 62 percent of parents of teenagers are unaware that their children view porn.

- 60 percent of all Web site visits are sexual in nature.

- The age at which the average U.S. male first sees Playboy or a similar magazine is 12.

- Americans spend an estimated $8-12 billion annually on pornography.

Porn is a huge problem, and one that the church, for the most part, is unaware of and uncomfortable dealing with today.

44

What is wrong with looking at porn?

Let's just list a few of the problems:

- Looking at porn increases the market for such material.

- Money that is dumped into the porn industry is used to promote more than just the porn industry alone. It also ends up supporting drug abuse, as well as violence.

- The porn industry is filled with victims of sexual molestation, and involvement in this business only deepens their pain.

- Porn has been shown to encourage viewers to commit sex-related crimes toward others.

- In relationships, looking at porn can cause problems because the porn becomes an unhealthy outlet.

- Porn is often the starting point for sexual addictions.

In short, porn destroys people, relationships, careers, and lives. Those are just a few of the fun things to look forward to when you take a walk down Porn Boulevard.

How much is too much porn?

That depends. My counter question is: How willing are you to potentially ruin your relationship with your spouse or future spouse? Perhaps looking at pornography has not affected you yet, but as time progresses, as life progresses—it's amazing how quickly so many men and women turn back to their "dabbling" in porn.

For example, a husband and wife get into an argument and instead of dealing with the situation, he decides to use porn as an outlet. It sounds stupid, but dabbling with this stuff is how addiction begins.

For the Christians who are reading this, I have another question: How do you feel about walking a tightrope without a net? We've met hundreds of people who have told us that pornography has led them to the lowest point of their life. Sin is fun for a season, but it has consequences!

I was talking to some young people about the age-old question: "How much sin can I have in my life and still be in good standing?" I told the group I was going to bake something to illustrate my point, and brought out a cart full of cooking materials and a plate of precooked brownies.

"Who wants a fudge brownie?" I yelled. In less than a minute, all the brownies were passed out and were being eagerly downed by the teen onlookers. As they finished the brownies, I began to demonstrate to them the recipe I'd used. I poured out the brownie mix, stirred in two eggs, and added a little white sugar and a smidgeon of brown sugar.

Then I paused and asked, "What if I were to tell you I added just a pinch of a special ingredient to the brownies you just ate? How many would want to know what it is?" I pulled the tin foil off the silver tray to reveal a large pile of dog poop. I took a spoon and dropped a tiny bit of poop in the pot, then stirred frantically. One student, who had eaten three brownies, was turning green in the front row. I sarcastically asked what was wrong. "It was just a *little*," I explained innocently. "Really, it bakes right out."

Of course, the brownies they had eaten were fine. I'd bought them at the store an hour earlier, and I told them that. But my point was made. How much dog poop does it take to ruin dessert? The answer—even the smallest amount will ruin a whole batch of brownies. 1 Corinthians 5:6 says, "Don't you know that a little yeast works through the whole batch of dough?"

Can porn be considered an art form?

The origin of the word porn comes from *pornea*, which is also the root for the word *prostitution*. Porn is dangerous because it feasts off our human desires—lust of the flesh and lust of the eyes.

46

The human body is an expression of God's greatest creation. We are God's canvas, or better yet, the beautiful artwork of God. The issue is how the body is used. It is not "art" to take something that was meant to be done by a married couple in private and exploit it to the public.

Because porn is so visually stimulating, rape, incest, and molestation are often the result of prolonged exposure to it. According to William Marshall, Ph.D., author of *A Report on the Use of Pornography by Sexual Offenders*, 87 percent of girl child molesters and 77 percent of boy child molesters admitted to regular use of hard-core pornography. Is that the result of art? We don't think so.

47

What does God think of porn stars?

God loves porn stars! WHAT? It may sound outrageous, but the Big Guy upstairs seems to have a thing for sinners—people who are missing out on his perfect will for their lives.

By no means are we saying that God is okay with the fact that people use their bodies in sexual acts for the direct purpose of selling explicit material to make a profit. But we believe that God desires for *all* people to know him and be united with him so he can give them something better—and yes, that's right, his plan includes porn stars! Jesus came for the sick, not for the healthy.

Take a look at John 8:1-11. Some religious folks dragged a prostitute up to Jesus and asked if they should stone her. Jesus' response was to tell this "woman of the night" to go and sin no more. I believe God offers the same invitation to "go and sin no more" to any porn star whose heart is open to his love. But those who are not open to God's love need to understand that they are ultimately going to face God's judgment if they don't turn their lives around. The most incredible thing about Jesus is that whether it's the president or a porn star, he loves them all the same.

I keep getting junk porn mail. I've never looked at any porn sites. How do I make the porn people stop sending me e-mails?

48   If you've been "spammed" by someone you don't know, do not reply to the sender or follow any removal instructions that might be included. Why? Because if you unsubscribe, you're telling the pornster that your e-mail address is working and they can then turn around and sell your address to other spamsters.

If you receive pornographic "spam," complain to the U.S. Attorney's office. Don't accuse anyone of a crime; just ask the office to investigate the porn spam as a possible violation of the Federal Obscenity Laws that prohibit the use of computers to transmit obscene material (18 USC 1462 and 1465). You should also complain to your Internet Service Provider (ISP), as well as to the sender's ISP. Most ISP administrators have policies that prohibit spamming through their accounts. Once they are notified that a user has been abusing their account, many ISPs will shut down the offender.

Additional information about dealing with spam is available from Abuse.net. Their home page at www.abuse.net has good links to other anti-spam resources.

PORNOGRAPHY AND THE INTERNET

The Internet can become a snare for me when it comes to porn, but I need it for e-mail and other positive things. Must I lose it, or should I just limit it?

We suggest downloading XXXchurch's free accountability software, X3watch, and see how that goes for a while. If you continue to struggle with looking at "hoochie mamas" online, then we say get rid of your Internet access altogether because it will eventually choke out the positive things.

In Matthew 5:27-30, Jesus said that if your hand causes you to stumble, then cut it off. If your eye causes you to stumble, then pluck it out. Obviously, this was a drastic example to communicate a straightforward principle. Jesus made it very clear that it would be better to eliminate all activities that cause us failure.

49

If your problem is beyond what accountability software can deal with, it is safe to say that the privilege of convenient Internet communication, such as e-mail or Instant Messaging, must cease. The positive things that the Internet can provide have been overloaded and hijacked by the negative effects of inappropriate material.

I found out that my brother visits 10 different porn sites a day. Do you have any pointers as to what I should say to try to get him to stop?

You shouldn't condemn your brother when you talk to him about this. Try to take it slow and easy the first time you approach him, or you will push him away and lose your credibility. Let him know that you are concerned about him. Ask him questions as to why he might be doing this, and let him try to explain. Try to find out why he uses porn for an escape and what he is escaping from. Then try to explain to him that porn is not healthy for him and his relationships with other people. You could suggest trying to get him hooked up with a strong Christian man who will help him to stay accountable.

As we've stated earlier, it is up to every individual to decide whether he or she really wants to live free and pure. Ultimately, if your brother does not want to change, you may only be able to pray for him and support him in the down times. But we firmly believe that wisdom is given to those who ask for it. When your brother gets fed up with his addictive and harmful behavior, he may begin to seek purity.

What if I like looking at gay porn? What do I do?

The basic concept is the same, whether it's gay porn or straight porn. Porn is porn no matter which way you cut it. The tools for avoiding it are the same, and the steps to overcome it work in both situations.

It's interesting to find that we have talked to a lot of straight or heterosexual guys who slowly got into gay porn. This falls in line with the natural progression of regular porn use. It starts with the *Sports Illustrated* swimsuit issue, then *Playboy*, and then suddenly you've progressed to loving gay porn!

So what do you do? Confess it to God. The Bible is the only thing that can clear out the harmful images that are on your mind's eye. Flush the toxins in your mind by filling it with the purity of the Word. The Bible will again make clear that God created you to fulfill his plans for your life. Porn, gay or straight, derails the purity that is his plan.

Are there any good books for single men about dealing with porn?

There are a number of excellent resources available via the XXXchurch Web site at www.xxxchurch.com. We'd also recommend *The Naked Truth* by Bill Perkins (available at www.invertbooks.com), *At the Altar of Sexual Idolatry* by Steve Gallagher (available from www.purelifeministries.org), and *Every Young Man's Battle* by Stephen Arterburn, Fred Stoeker, and Mike Yorkey (available from www.everyyoungmansbattle.com).

I am a Christian girl who has been dabbling in pornography for years. It is definitely my "dirty little secret." I want to come clean to my fiancé, family, and friends. How do I talk about this with the most important people in my life?

You should tell your fiancé before you get married. There will not be an easy way for you to tell him. You must find a time and place where you can both talk without distractions and be honest with him. More than likely, he will understand and want to help you be free. I would also recommend that if you are being physical with your boyfriend, you stop for the remainder of your engagement.

It is also important that you find another woman with whom you can talk about this—someone you trust who won't condemn you, but will help you to be accountable. Beyond that, it is up to you as to how many of your friends and family you talk with about this. If you believe they will help you be free and

QUESTIONS YOU CAN'T ASK YOUR MAMA ABOUT SEX

accountable, then tell them. But if you are getting help from a few good people and making progress, I don't think you need to tell everyone you know.

The important thing is to get God involved in your road to freedom. Please don't let any guilt and shame from this keep you away from God. He wants you to ask for his help so you will be free.

People are asking me to have cyber-sex. Is that okay?

Cyber-sex is just another form of selfish sexual expression. It will leave you hanging—always wanting more and never satisfied. People who tend to dabble with cyber-sex typically are not where they want to be. Usually they desire some form of relationship with a person of the opposite sex and this is as close as they can get, so they venture into it.

Cyber-sex is dangerous because it often leads to more destructive forms of sexual expression. You may say to yourself, "No way, it won't happen to me," but you should read some of the e-mails we've received. People get more and more needy, and they find themselves getting in deeper and deeper as they seek out alternate forms of sexual gratification. Why put yourself in that situation?

And who really knows what kind of person is on the other side of that cyber-conversation? Sure, the screen name may be "sexygrl22," but chances are really good that people offering cyber-sex are not who they say they are. They could be married. They may say they are the same age as you and a member of the opposite sex, when in reality they could be that old, fat, sweaty guy from across the street. The fantasy of the cyber-world allows people to deceive others into believing they are someone they are not.

Chapter Four

Lust

*I want
them nude,
NOW!*

There are a lot of attractive girls out there, and sometimes my mind wanders and I have unwanted fantasies about them. What can I do to curb the sexual thoughts I have about these girls?

The Bible says to take captive every thought. Even the apostle Paul said he had to bring every thought into submission of God's perspective—which may be of some comfort to us as we wrestle through this maze of social development.

As you recognize that the beauty of the opposite sex is a gift from God, refrain from fantasy. The enemy wants to keep the battle a mental one. Usually we are weak on the mental battlefield because it's easy to slip by keeping our thoughts to ourselves.

57

We would suggest prayer and Bible reading, and maybe adding some of your favorite Christian music to the mix. Music can transform your environment as well as your emotions. Also, as you can imagine, it's difficult to fantasize while singing about the love of Jesus. If this doesn't help, ask a guy that you trust to keep you accountable, really accountable.

It seems like sexual material is all around us in this culture. How do you flee from something that is everywhere you turn?

Dealing with the amount of sexually suggestive themes running through our culture can be problematic. Fighting those daily battles requires identifying the sources that tend to be the most tempting for you.

For example, let's say the local magazine rack tends to be a distraction for you. Whenever you go to grab the latest issue of *Guitar Player*, you always find yourself grabbing a copy of this week's *Maxim* magazine featuring "Ten Ways to Increase Your Sex Drive" and the special lingerie pin-up section. If you recognize that the magazine rack is a problem for you, then think of ways to avoid it. Get a subscription to *Guitar Player* so you never have to leave your house to buy the magazine.

Why do I still have trouble lusting over pictures and videos I've seen in the past?

58

Imagine your mind as a giant canvas. Everything you see, hear, or experience is painted on this canvas in your mind. You continue to see and experience "flashbacks" because these images have been etched into your conscience. These vivid images can only go away with God's intervention.

In the New Testament, Paul urges that we should "renew our minds daily." What he was saying is that we need to allow God's paintbrushes to repaint our canvases with images of his perfect will for our lives. His artistic expression will redefine the images of our past defilements until our minds once again reflect the image of the pure hearts we seek.

When you are tempted to fantasize, ask God for help in that very moment. Don't focus on the fantasy; focus on other things. Go do something or hang out with someone to get your mind off of it. If you only focus on not doing it, you will probably end up doing it.

I keep going back to the same sin—lust. I don't know how to get rid of it or how to stop lusting. What should I do?

Lust always comes from a source, so the best practical advice we can give you is for you to think about and write out a list of everything that may cause you to lust. Then pray that God will plan ways to help you avoid or get rid of those areas of temptation.

For example, if computer porn is always tempting you, then you need to get rid of Internet access. Or if magazines, even the ones like *Stuff* or *Maxim*, make you distracted, then make a commitment to stay out of the magazine sections in stores. I know some of these suggestions may sound harsh, but if you truly want to live a lust-free life, then you must take drastic measures to stop things before they even begin.

Also, take some time to read 1 John. It specifically defines the issues with the lust of the flesh and the lust of the eyes. These are root sins that produce horrible fruit. Both lusts can consume who you are and heavily influence your actions. In your case, they are forcing you into repetitious actions that you want to change.

I want to suggest that you reflect on a few more Scripture passages. Take a look at John 6:63; Romans 13:14; and 1 John 2:15-17. Dive into the Bible and allow it to flush out the sexual toxins that have poisoned you.

I want to do the right thing, but I always do what is wrong. Help me!

The apostle Paul knew exactly what you are talking about. Take a look at these words from Romans 7:16-17 (*NLT*): "I know perfectly well that what I am doing is wrong, and my bad conscience shows that I agree that the law is good. But I can't help myself, because it is sin inside me that makes me do these evil things."

The first step is to confess your problem to God. You may have tried this before and it didn't work, or maybe you've never mentioned it to God. First things first: Know that God loves and forgives you and wants to be in right relationship with you.

The second step is to confess it to someone else. Most people never do this. Porn is the "dirty little secret," and that is why it will never go away. You can't overcome an addiction to sin by yourself.

The third step is to clean it up! Take practical steps so you don't return to doing the very thing that you hate. You know where your struggles happen and what you can do. Quit making excuses. Today is the day to be honest with yourself, honest with God, and honest with others.

Chapter Five

Masturbation
Cold showers and open doors

What is your stance—and God's stance—on masturbation?

We have received literally thousands of e-mails about this particular issue. We have heard all the scenarios, "Well, if I think about fruit while I'm masturbating, then it's not a sin." Isn't that clever? Or "If I'm giving glory to the Lord while I'm doing it, then that can't be wrong, right?" Hmmm, why don't we just make that part of our Sunday morning services, then?

Our stance reflects our interpretation of God's perspective on purity as it's rooted in the Scriptures. Granted, nowhere does it say, "Thou shalt not masturbate." However, it does say in many passages to keep your mind clean, pure, and holy.

63

God also calls us to sacrifice our own bodily desires. Paul said it this way: "I die daily." He is saying that our own desires must be crucified each day in order to fulfill God's desires for our lives. I have never met anyone who can honestly say that his mind is meditating on pure things while he is pleasuring themselves.

Others have said, "Well, it's better to masturbate than to burn with lust." That is like saying it's better to steal a car than to have an affair. The whole argument is flawed because one self-serving act is replacing another. Here's the truth: If you want to live a life that honors God, then start pleasing him and stop pleasing yourself. Stop making excuses and get some control over your life. Yes, it is tough. Yes, we know the hormones are raging. However, God is calling us to holiness.

Do you lose your virginity with masturbation?

We have never claimed to be the smartest guys on the planet. But after years of schooling and all those James Dobson tapes my parents made me listen to, I think I can safely say that the answer to your question is a big NO! But as we've said, the issue is not virginity, but purity. Although you won't lose your virginity by masturbating, you do lose aspects of purity. One should not be seen as having more or less value than the other. God gave both of them to you and they should be cherished equally. I have seen so many people who maintain their virginity by definition, yet live a hedonistic lifestyle.

In Psalm 24, God urges us to seek purity. Unfortunately, it is one of the very few things in this world that is given away too freely, despite the fact that it is priceless.

Does masturbation have any emotional, physical, or sexual side effects?

We get this kind of question a lot. Now, maybe your parents told you that if you touched yourself "down there," you would grow hair on your palms or your little private would fall off. You know that's not true. But here are some things to think about:

1. Masturbation brings emotional baggage. You feel like a turd and you feel guilty about doing it. You've got secrets, and you spend a lot of time hiding what you're doing.

2. Masturbation is all about pleasing you, instead of the Lord.

3. Do you think your future wife wants a husband who does it four times a day?

Masturbation is kind of like a coin that Satan places in front of us as bait. At first it appears to have value and worth. But as we reach out to grab it, he flips the coin on us, and the reverse side contains guilt, pain, lust, and so on.

The Bible calls us to be holy because God is holy (1 Peter 1:16). God calls us to decrease our desires, so his presence in us can increase (John 3:30). And only good things can come from that exchange.

Can you give practical advice on handling lust before it demands masturbation?

Avoid things that you know will lead to lust, thus making masturbation a non-issue. If you know being left alone with your computer will lead you to lust, then avoid the Internet or don't have a computer. (You know, many people used to live without computers back in the good old days.) If you start to lust when you watch a movie that has questionable content, avoid those movies. If you stay up late and masturbate, go to bed early. If you masturbate in the shower, take a cold one. If you masturbate in bed, leave the door open.

The bottom line is to guard your life and don't believe the lie that says you can never be successful. The Bible makes it very clear that God is not a tempter. In Mark 14:38, Jesus tells his disciples, "Watch and pray so that you will not fall into temptation. The spirit is willing, but the body is weak." Instead, God will provide you a trap door to escape through when you are tempted. When you are feeling tempted, look for the way out that God is providing for you. You may be amazed at the results. Sometimes, in searching for a way out, the attention you were giving to an inappropriate image will be redirected to a healthy alternative.

I remember talking to a teen once about this issue. In searching for a way out, he made a commitment to go running and exercise whenever he felt tempted. After many months of working out instead of lingering in the land of lust, this young man was in tremendous shape—not only physically, but also spiritually. Get the picture? Do anything you can to stay away from the things that make you lust!

Plus, think of the kittens!

Does God really kill a kitten every time you masturbate?

Yes, he does. Okay, no, he doesn't. Someone once sent us an e-mail about this urban legend, and we decided to start a whole campaign on our Web site around the idea that God kills a kitten every time someone masturbates. The point was to help people (particularly *church* people) find a way to begin talking about the issue of masturbation.

Masturbation is a difficult word that often brings with it various presuppositions. Many people in the church find the word to be terribly negative and offensive. The minute the topic comes up, many folks go into denial mode, especially if they masturbate frequently in secret, and even more so if that activity is tied into a pornography addiction.

It might seem silly, but we have found that people are able to talk far more freely about "killing kittens" than about masturbation directly. Somehow it doesn't feel as threatening to admit to having killed one or two kittens once or twice a week. The important thing to understand is that "killing kittens" is a means to opening a safe space for conversation on the subject; it's a doorway to the room, not the room itself.

I want to respect my girlfriend and her desire that we not sleep together. Is masturbating my only form of release?

No. You may think it is your only form of physical release, but to think this is to believe that you can out-plan God. You won't die if you don't service yourself. Our all-knowing God did not overlook the fact that the male body may need to get rid of semen that is not used.

During adolescence, most young men become acquainted with the nocturnal emission, also known as a "wet dream." While sleeping, the body relaxes and semen is emitted through the penis. The small ejaculate alleviates this so-called "need" for a release.

Renowned Christian speakers and thinkers have lined up on both sides of the table with regard to whether it's okay to masturbate. It's possible that those who argue it's no big deal to "release one" have built that argument to condone their own struggles. Others who rail against masturbation and judgmentally bash those who admit their struggles with the issue may be doing so only to appear holy in their own area of weakness.

We believe you need to look not at masturbation itself but at the cause. If the "Big M" is the fruit on the tree, then what is the root issue? Often, it's lust. I've never met anyone who took pride in the fact that he could pleasure himself and still keep his mind focused on the things of God. Masturbation is often part of a thought life that has escaped to the fantasyland of sexual escapades.

Jesus once said that a man who looks lustfully upon a woman has already committed adultery with her in his heart (Matthew 5:27-28). Was he saying that thoughts and actions are the same? No. He was saying that thoughts, over time, lead to actions. Most people who masturbate are reliant on unhealthy thoughts, videos, porn, or other sexually explicit material—all of it outside of God's perfect will for the Christian life. So address the root cause of the actions.

There are two other critical pieces to keep in mind: forgiveness and freedom. First, if you have a problem with masturbation, find forgiveness! As with every area of life where we miss the mark, we must address the sin quickly, but not bury ourselves in condemnation. There is no "greater sin" with God. Sin is sin. Jesus died for all sin. The only sin that God will not address is hidden or unforgiven sin.

Second, fight for freedom! If you are currently struggling in this area, don't just say, "It owns me." Fight. Determine a path to wholeness. Take drastic measures if you need to. Do whatever it takes because the longer you wait, the more deadly it becomes. Remember the power of your vision. The Bible says your eyes will never be satisfied. Your eyes will always want more. Allow God to set you free.

Chapter Six

Sexual Addiction

*Hardcore
hang-ups*

I'm a sixteen-year-old male and I have the age-old problem of porn. Every time I get online, I'm attracted to banner ads and I always get sucked in. Do you know of any way that I can break myself of this?

The first thing you can do, if you really want to stop, is to put your computer in the kitchen and only go online when your mom is cooking meals. I would bet money that you won't be tempted to click on any nudie sites while mom is making dinner. If this is too hard for you, then get rid of your computer altogether.

If you must have a computer, try downloading our accountability software, X3watch. When you do so, you'll need to enter the e-mail address of a person (or persons) who will periodically receive a listing of the Web sites you've looked at recently. Sign up your mom as well as a friend or pastor. I wouldn't want to be at your house when your mom sees a report with porn sites on it!

In addition, XXXchurch has partnered with Integrity Online, the nation's largest filtered Internet provider, to provide clean Internet access. Sign up today at www.integrity.com.

Can you be born a sex addict?

Studies have shown that addictive personalities tend to run in families. Now, you can debate the old argument of Nature versus Nurture over and over, but we think there is a more important factor to discuss here—choice.

Each of us has been given the ability to choose and to make wise decisions. We are not robots programmed for sex addiction. Some people may have a greater tendency to become addicted to sex, drugs, or other stuff like that, but the bottom line is that each of us has a choice.

Let's quit living below the level that God has called us to and blaming our genes for the choices we make. It is not based on our heritage. It is not based on our ethnicity. It is rooted in sin. It is important to remember that we're human beings who can practice self-control.

I have been addicted to porn for five years. I have read self-help books, prayed, read the Word, told my girlfriend, and even asked my pastor to keep me accountable. Is there anything else you can suggest?

Consider the big difference between the following statements: "Lord, take this from me," and "Lord, I give this to you." It may seem like interpretation stuff, but in reality it can make a huge difference. God desires to give us whole and abundant lives. How much better is it when we willfully offer to give our desires and failures to him?

God will not reach out of heaven and try to pry our fingers off our sin. That would invalidate the free will we've been given. Yet he is quick to take on our failure if we are willing to give it to him. Remain encouraged, because Psalm 51:7 reminds us that God can purify us and make us "whiter than snow."

I'd urge you to continue to be accountable to people you trust, because when you bring the problem into the light, it takes a lot of the power of the temptation away. If that doesn't work, cut your hands off; you can probably get decent money for them on eBay.

When it's late at night and I feel tempted to go to a porn site instead of seeking God, how do I stop myself from being weak one more time?

Proverb 26:11 *(NIRV)* says, "A foolish person who does the same foolish things again is like a dog that returns to where it has thrown up." I suggest getting a dog so this verse will become clearer for you. When you watch that stupid dog puke and then suck up the vomit over and over again, you will get upset at the dog. Remember, God doesn't get upset with us when we go back to our sin; it saddens him, because he loves us and wants the best for us.

73

It's important that you don't let yourself be alone late at night and allow yourself to flirt with the idea of going to these Web sites. If you live alone and know this tempts you, then take care of the problem by getting rid of your computer. If you absolutely cannot do this, you need to put our free accountability software—X3watch—on your computer so that whomever agreed to hold you accountable will receive an e-mail that lists all the questionable sites you looked at in a month. Start getting real and accountable with someone.

Why do men seem to have this problem more than women do?

Well, one reason is because men tend to be sexually aroused through visual stimulation, while women tend to become aroused through emotional stimulation. Obviously, pornography is *very* visually stimulating.

QUESTIONS YOU CAN'T ASK YOUR MAMA ABOUT SEX

But we have recognized that pornography and sexual addictions are not just a male problem, and we are seeking to address this issue more and more on our Web site and our ministry. There is now a whole section geared toward women on our site, and a campaign called NoHo.

NoHo talks about what women can do to help provide more solutions, not more problems. We are also working with some female speakers who address issues of sexual purity and appearance, and sometimes they join us on the X3tour. (For more information on this, check out the X3tour page on the site.)

Guys are more visual then girls, but over the last year we have talked to many women who are fighting this battle. We will keep addressing this topic for you girls.

What can the church do to help those who are struggling with sexual addiction?

First, the church needs to get educated. There are many people who take a negative stance toward the church due to its lack of vulnerability when addressing the subject. Some say things like, "The church goes poking its big nose around, making all kinds of assumptions, and shooting off its mouth before getting the facts." This creates division.

The church needs to see those who are addicted to pornography not as freaks or perverts, but as people who struggle. Church members need to get a deeper awareness of the nature of the problem and create supportive groups where people can openly discuss this issue. As we noted earlier, in a recent study 37 percent of pastors admitted to struggling with porn. Of course, this study was anonymous because most of these pastors don't have the guts to tell their congregation about their real-life struggles. And that is tragic! How many more people could we reach if our pastors were open and honest? Wouldn't that make their congregations want to do the same?

There is another thought that needs to be addressed with regard to the church. Remember who the church is. The church is not a building, but people. The church is you and me. What can we do better? Let me suggest three points to consider:

1. Be committed to prayer.

2. Be compassionate and care for those who struggle with this issue, even if you do not.

3. Share the message of hope that there is life beyond an addiction to porn.

When we embrace these truths as the church, people will find the freedom the Bible promises.

Chapter Seven
Accountability

*No more dirty
little secrets*

I keep hearing how I should "be accountable" to someone with my life and relationships. But truthfully, I have no idea what this means or how it works.

Accountability is a great concept that is often made way too complex and difficult. In its simplest definition, accountability is having someone partner with you to support and encourage you to make the right decisions when faced with tough issues. A second part of the accountability process is that it ensures you have someone who will stay in tune with you after you have faced a decision.

Let me describe it this way: Suppose I am a teen. A friend and I are playing a video game on the Net. We get this wild idea to search out some topic. While we are searching, we come across some inappropriate links. Our curiosity is stirring, and I ask him if we should click to the site. As we both consider it, accountability comes alive. Because there are two of us making the decision, and because we have committed to seeking God's best not only for ourselves but also for each other, my friend says, "This isn't a good idea. Let's go shoot some hoops instead." He was a strong voice of reason in the midst of a tempting decision. That's what accountability looks like before a bad decision is made.

What about after a tough decision? Suppose my girlfriend and I decide to go out on a date. At the end of the evening, we decide to pull off the road so we can talk. As we are chatting, things heat up and we mess around and go further than we wanted to go. The next day my accountability friend calls me and asks how the date went. When he asks if I honored my commitment to purity, I tell him I did not. Rather than judging me, he asks me where I went wrong and what I can do next time to prevent the same mistakes. He challenges me and encourages me to keep my behavior in alignment with my beliefs.

To take accountability seriously is to invite someone into your life who will assist you and support you on your tough decisions. It needs to be someone you respect and someone you will listen to.

Most of the time, the reason we avoid accountability is that we don't want anyone in our business. There's only one problem: You have to decide whether you want privacy or purity. I have never met anyone who had guarded privacy yet could also maintain a guaranteed purity.

My friend is sleeping with her boyfriend. What should I do?

Your friend is making choices that affect her life. It is admirable that you want to help her, but if she does not want to help herself, all you can do is be a strong and consistent support. Until she decides to change, your physical role is limited. So stay in tune spiritually.

First, always speak the truth gently. Sometimes what another person needs to do is so apparent to us that we speak it bluntly. However, a soft word may draw her into a conversation that could lead to a decision to change.

Secondly, speak with compassion. There are often deep issues that are associated with seeking fulfillment from sexual promiscuity. Compassion will help you to see the greater needs she has. You can help her by offering kindness and compassion.

Finally, when she is ready to talk about her desire to change, be ready to listen. Refrain from the "I told you so" speech.

All of the above must be wrapped in daily prayer. The following is an example of how to pray for her: "Lord, I am praying for my friend ————————. God, I ask you to reveal to her the plan that you have for her life. Show her that she can find fulfillment in your Word. Show her that purity can be restored. I ask you to strengthen her to the point of making a change. Give to her the discernment she needs in order to know what to do each day." This is a simple but effective way to communicate with God on her behalf.

You've talked about downloading your X3watch software as an accountability tool to help me stay away from porn on the Internet. How does it work?

On its own our X3watch software won't prevent you from looking at porn on the Internet. But what it *can* do is force you to be more accountable for your actions.

When you download the software, you will be asked to enter one or more e-mail addresses into the program. The person or persons whose e-mails you enter will serve as accountability partners for you. Each of them will get a listing of the Web sites you've looked at recently. Sign up your pastor, a friend, your mom or dad—anyone who supports you in your commitment to avoid porn.

Accountability is real. It is deep, not shallow. It is brutally honest and requires trust on both sides. We suggest you disclose to someone you respect, admire, and are open to sharing with on a regular basis. This person must be strong enough to confront you and spiritual enough to support you when you are struggling.

X3watch is not an end-all solution. It's similar to a lock. It will make failure more difficult. It will make it harder to seek porn. Why? Because you know your buddy will be able to expose you and call you on the carpet. But even the best "locks of accountability" can be navigated around. You can put a thousand-dollar lock on a ten-dollar door, but it won't guarantee success. There are many people who will try to find a way around the system. If that is the case, have at it! The sincerity is questionable and failure inevitable.

How is accountability supposed to work? Should it be a daily thing, or what?

We'd recommend that you and your accountability partner talk every few days. That should help you get on the road to success. It's also important that you be able to talk to each other in the moment that you or your partner are being tempted to do something you will regret, even if it's in the middle of the night. Be in contact often enough that you can be active in each other's lives and pray and believe in the best for your friend.

I stopped downloading X3watch when it asked me to put in a friend's e-mail address. I want to stop looking at porn, but I don't want anyone to know. What should I do?

Good luck getting rid of porn by yourself. It won't happen. That's why it's the dirty little secret—because no one knows. You need to tell someone. Accountability is not possible if no one else knows about your situation.

I'm not sure what you believe accountability to be, but please consider the possibility that you have a misunderstanding of its purpose. Our Web site exists to get you on your way to talking about your problem; our software works with an accountability partner to help you maintain integrity while you are online.

I do have accountability partners in my life, yet the struggle to look at porn still remains. Is there an application that makes it impossible to view porn via the Internet?

The struggle is always going to be there. Since the Garden of Eden, humanity has been infused with the temptation to sin. What complicates the issue is the devious nature of porn. Porn is secret and seductive. It feeds off the lust nature of wanting more because the "eyes will never be satisfied." When we are struggling with a moral challenge, and especially if we have failed the test, our nature is to run and hide. Adam and Eve did the same thing— they tried to hide from God. Can you imagine that? They tried to hide their sin in the same way that porn is hidden, creating the dirty little secret.

83

The next time you are being tempted and acting out, you need to run to God and say, "I need help in a bad way." And utilize your accountability partner; call that person every day if you have to. But most importantly, please believe more in God's ability to set you free than in the enemy's ability to keep you in bondage.

I am trying really hard to stay away from porn, but I'm hanging on by a thread. I don't have anyone I can be accountable to because my best friend thinks porn is okay and another friend I have would be too disgusted for me to discuss this problem with him.

Remember what happened to Pee Wee Herman? Everyone loved him and thought he was great on TV until he—well, we all know what happened. PORN! Quit believing the lie that it's okay and that you can't stop it. You are headed down Porn Boulevard, where everyone crashes.

84   I think you need to find some new friends. It is important that you find someone you can trust who will help you to be accountable. Friends should be there to sharpen you, rather than to destroy you. Proverbs 27:6 talks about how a wound from a friend is better than a kiss from an enemy. Consider the influence your friends' perspectives are having on you. Their attitudes are causing you to weaken, rather than grow stronger. Your friendships may feel like a kiss of social influence; but in reality, they are destructive. Establish friendships that will enhance your pursuit of purity.

Chapter Eight

Everything but the Kitchen Sink

You mean there's more?

What kind of sex does God consider okay in a marriage?

The Bible doesn't say what kind of sexual activity is okay and what isn't, as long as it is inside a marriage relationship. Remember that God made sex to be enjoyed, and he made us to be creative beings. So if both people are consenting—and it is pleasurable for both people—then there shouldn't be anything wrong with nontraditional sex.

Of course you need to think about (and find out if you're unsure) whether or not certain methods of sex are going to cause long-term harm to your partner, even if your spouse enjoys it. After all, you don't want to engage in forms of sex that could be potentially dangerous—that would be a blatant case of not taking care of your partner!

87

Is it wrong for married couples to use sex toys?

This is a question we get often, and I'm sure there are a lot of different opinions about it. Our answer: If it is beneficial and edifying to you, your partner, and the Lord, then go for it!

I would offer one caution, though. A lot of couples try bringing pornography and stuff like that into their sexual relationship, and that, I would say, is not a good thing. In fact, it is a recipe for disaster. But we think toys, lotions, and other things that are meant to please your spouse are okay—as long as they're not potentially dangerous to one or both partners or likely to cause permanent damage in the long run.

Keep in mind that whips, chains, or being overly rough during sex is often a sign that some sort of abuse may have taken place in the past. In these situations, some counseling may be in order.

I think I am pregnant. I don't know how it happened. I was told I could not get pregnant if it was my first time. How can I hide this from my parents?

I'm sorry you were given such bad information regarding the possibility of getting pregnant your first time. This is the type of confusion that causes people to make inappropriate decisions. However, the greater issue is not how you got pregnant, but that you want to hide this matter from your parents.

It is understandable that you would be apprehensive about telling them truth. That is a normal fear. It's likely that they will be disappointed in your situation, scared for your future, and may not be able to trust you to make the right decisions for a while. It will be a difficult time. But being pregnant does not cause God to love you any less. He loves you more now than ever, and he loves the child that is developing inside of you, too. I encourage you to confess your past wrongs and mistakes to God, and then move beyond them and get back into a healthy decision-making process.

The first good decision you need to make right now is to begin taking the best possible care of the child inside of you. To do this, you need to tell your parents—and his parents—about this immediately. If you need to take a youth pastor, teacher, coach, or trusted adult with you for support, that's great. But tell them today! They need to know so they can assist you with the next step.

Second, schedule a doctor's appointment today. Let the doctor examine your health and the baby's. Prenatal vitamins, ultrasounds, governmental medical assistance for mothers and children, and possible insurance coverage are all elements that your folks need to help you with as soon as possible. And if they won't help you, find someone who will!

Finally, ask God for health and strength. Acknowledge that you missed the mark. Get beyond the past by committing and dedicating this child to God. He will lead you and guide you in every step of the journey.

When you think about all of this today, I know it seems overwhelming. And God knows it's overwhelming. This feeling of desperation is just one of the feelings that God wanted to protect you from by establishing his instructions for purity. On the other hand, the enemy will try to convince you that you will never succeed and you will never live a normal life. This is FALSE! There are many women, men, and children who were adversely affected by an unplanned pregnancy and still succeeded in accomplishing their goals and dreams. Will it be easy? No. Is it possible? Yes! Will you succeed? YES.

Our prayers are with you and your child.

I'm 15, a Christian, and I'm also a homosexual. Why would God make me gay?

We are all born into this world as jacked-up creatures. Church people like to use the term "sin nature," but let's use the word "jacked-up." Deep down, we all want to please ourselves, and doing the wrong thing comes naturally.

Now, I don't want to go down the "homosexuality is a sin" road, because we have all heard that a thousand times. I do want to say that, in God's eyes, sin is sin. I don't care what your sexual orientation is, and I don't think God does either. He just looks down from heaven and sees his children in need of his mercy and forgiveness every day. You've got baggage. I've got baggage. Welcome to the club. But I believe that God did not *make* you gay, just like Adam did not have to eat the apple.

You must remember, even though the church has made homosexuality its pet sin to hate, God is a lover of people. God created you in HIS IMAGE. How can a person be created gay? Sure, there are cases when a chemical imbalance causes a man or woman to a have some traits that usually belong to the opposite sex—but that is a chemical imbalance or deficiency, just as diabetes is. The imbalance needs to be addressed from a medical perspective. But this is rare.

Homosexuality is a choice, as with any other sin, and often it is the result of social conditioning and a heart that has submitted to self-indulgence. The second half of Romans chapter 1 speaks clearly to this. As with any sin pattern, repentance and restoration is the hope. God did not create the human body to function properly in same-sex relationships. Please do not corrupt the perfection of God's plan by declaring that he made you that way. If you are willing to address these issues, contact Exodus Ministries (exodus-international.org).

I am scared that I may have gotten a sexually transmitted disease. I had sex with a guy who was just overheard telling others that he has an STD.

First of all, there's a chance the guy may have been lying about it. In a sick way, he may think that talking about having a sexually transmitted disease would somehow make him seem cool. The last time I checked, bragging about an STD was not high on the cool list, but nothing is surprising anymore.

It's difficult to answer this—I can already feel the hot breath of some religious folks who would love to scream at me about how offering you any kind of proactive help is somehow condoning your mistakes. That is the furthest thing from the truth. Let me be clear. The fact that you may have been exposed to an STD is the consequence of sin. STDs are the result of people not honoring their bodies or the wishes of the Creator of their bodies. Had you not been "down under," you wouldn't have to worry about whether or not you may have contracted an STD. But I believe it is tremendously important that we in the Christian community do not isolate or shun people because of a sticky subject matter.

The Centers for Disease Control (CDC) notes that:

There are two primary ways that STDs can be transmitted. Human immunodeficiency virus (HIV), as well as gonorrhea, chlamydia, and trichomoniasis—the discharge diseases—are transmitted when infected semen or vaginal fluids contact mucosal surfaces (e.g., the male urethra, the vagina or cervix). In contrast, genital ulcer diseases—genital herpes, syphilis, and chancroid—and human papillomavirus are primarily transmitted through contact with infected skin or mucosal surfaces.

All of those big words are a fancy way of saying that if you mess around, you are susceptible to getting an STD. At this point most argue, "But my boyfriend (girlfriend) is clean!" Well, that may be true. But you need to remember the mathematical factor: When you have sex with someone, you are exposed to every person they have been with, and every person that those people have been with, and on and on and on.

There are many different types of diseases that he may have passed to you. Go to God and ask him to make right what you have made wrong. One of the ways he may do this is by giving a doctor the insight to clear up your situation. As serious as the physical illness may be, I am just as concerned about the damage done to your emotions and spirit in this process. Take care of yourself by letting God lead and love you. He is not up in heaven trying to take away your fun. He is directing your path away from the elements on this earth that are the result of a broken covenant with him. Don't blame God. Don't blame anyone. Just refocus and recommit your ways to his ways.

I've heard that if I use a condom, I'm protected from AIDS. If this is true, then how does AIDS keep spreading?

This is a tough question to do justice to in such a small space, but let me give a brief overview. Here's the truth: The only complete protection from acquiring AIDS through sexual activity is abstinence. Millions of teenagers believe that the "Jimmy Cap" is a sure-fire way to protect people from AIDS. Though condoms have been proven to drastically reduce AIDS transmission, they surely are not foolproof. Science tells us otherwise.

Think of a condom as a series of mesh strands of rubber woven together. The mesh forms a tightly connected maze that resembles a fishing net. The problem is this: AIDS (and other STDs) are very small organisms, much smaller than sperm, which is what the condom was designed to stop. According to www. prolife.com/CONDOMS.html, the HIV virus that causes AIDS is so small that two million of the disease-causing agents could crowd onto the period at the end of a sentence. The distance between each woven strand is 50-450 times larger than the size of the AIDS virus. And it is possible for the AIDS virus to slip through the mesh holes (called voids) in a condom. (For more on this, see "Vatican: Condoms Don't Stop AIDS" by Steve Bradshaw, The Guardian UK, October 9, 2003, www.guardian. co.uk/aids/story/0,7369,1059068,00.html.)

If that isn't enough, consider what these medical physicians are saying:

> Simply put, condoms fail. And condoms fail at a rate unacceptable for me as a physician to endorse them as a strategy to be promoted as meaningful AIDS protection.
> —Dr. Robert Renfield, chief of retro-viral research, Walter Reed Army Institute

> You just can't tell people it's all right to do whatever you want as long as you wear a condom. [AIDS] is just too dangerous a disease to say that.
> —Dr. Harold Jaffee, chief of epidemiology, National Centers for Disease Control

> Saying that the use of condoms is "safe sex" is in fact playing Russian roulette. A lot of people will die in this

dangerous game.

—Dr. Teresa Crenshaw, member of the U.S. Presidential AIDS Commission and past president of the American Association of Sex Educators

Shifting from science to our faith, consider that God created us to live according to a higher standard. I'm not into Russian roulette, and I surely don't want to trust something that doctors won't trust. The Bible says to put your trust in God. And if God has my trust, then I have to trust that his Word offers the complete and undeniably best path for my life—God calls us to sexual purity and abstinence.

94

I went to prom last year. At the end of the night my boyfriend and I had sex. I hated it. I kept saying, "No, no, stop, quit it." As he held me down and finished, I cried. I feel horrible and dirty. What do I do?

You were raped. Date rape is still rape. Society has fallen into the trap of believing that if the girl says no, she really means yes. When you said no, the date should have been over. Too many times I have seen or heard comments from the church like, "Well, she shouldn't have been there," or "She let it go too far!" Wrong. Why do we bring reproach and accusation on the victim?

I probably should not assume this, but please, please, please tell me you dropped this guy off at the local sheriff's station and severed all ties. Secondly, I encourage you to go to the doctor with your parent(s) or guardian and have a complete medical check-up. Forced entry can do serious physical and emotional damage. A parent, trusted adult, or pastor can counsel you about the legal side of this. It may not be your first choice to press charges, but this guy could do the same thing to other girls, and he must be stopped.

In addition, you should get continuing counseling and support that will help establish health for your immediate future. Many women who have been raped either sever all ties to the opposite sex or completely give themselves over to sexual activity, thinking, *I might as well just sleep around, since I'm already dirty.* Both of these mindsets are off, and counseling can help remedy such feelings.

I am alarmed that this kind of thing happens nearly as often in the Christian culture as it does in the secular. Christian guys pressure girls to go further than they want to go, assuming that it's always the woman's responsibility to say no. And it is tragic, but true, that many times the "no" is not respected. The idea that any guy would think he is entitled to sex—or a blowjob, or even a kiss—needs to be addressed! Guys, if this is your attitude, the only thing you will be entitled to is the judgment God will bring down on you!

Sadly, the lack of respect for women is a huge issue among many teenage Christian boys, and it leads to a lot of messed up sexual activity. Sexual misconduct is everywhere in our culture, and many Christians have a distorted understanding regarding strong male leadership and female submission, which only makes this issue more dangerous. During my Christian college experience, I knew a lot of "great Christian guys" who were total sleazes toward their girlfriends. And I know way too many Christian girls who have experienced such unacceptable behavior.

As a father, I think of my daughter and cringe. Trying to even imagine my daughter being violated by some boy brings a righteous anger within me. Imagine how God must feel when this happens to one of his children. He sees every rape. As a Father, he is there to comfort, heal, and mend that which has been broken. I hope and pray that you will feel God's healing presence in the days ahead.

I've seen some pretty racy music videos lately. Do you think kids should even listen to music that isn't specifically Christian, since many of the videos are so bad?

If this is your biggest concern, you can take a deep breath and relax. Just make sure you don't play any music backwards—we've heard it could be Satanic!

There are some Christians who think any music that doesn't say "Jesus" is bad. Music is everywhere, and we love a lot of music you will never hear in a church. Just because the lyrics are not about Jesus doesn't mean we shouldn't let ourselves enjoy it.

However, a lot of the music videos on MTV and the music played on the radio are foul, inappropriate, and all about sex. When I was in seventh grade, my youth pastor took away my Van Halen tape. I got so mad that I didn't go back to church for a few years. But it did make me think more about the stuff I was listening to.

Fortunately, there are more great music groups for you to listen to today. Some of the music we would recommend includes PAX 217, Paul Wright, Subseven, Pillar, Jason Harwell, Number One Gun, Blindside, P.O.D., and Switchfoot.

It isn't practical to think you will only listen to Christian music. If that is your view, you need to throw out "Happy

Birthday" and "The Star-Spangled Banner" as well. Obviously, those are extreme examples, but the point remains the same.

What do you think about tattoos?

We think tattoos are an individual's preference. We *would* strongly advise you not to put the name of any girlfriend or boyfriend on your body. I know you might be deeply and madly in love now, but don't do it. Millions of people have made this mistake over the centuries, and they have experienced very painful surgery to remove the name of their exes from their bodies.

97

But beyond the trendy social risk of tattoos, if you are a teenager, consider your parents' perspective. The bigger issue is whether or not you are able to honor your parents' desires by getting a tattoo. The Bible does not say, "Thou shall not get a tattoo." But it does say that your body is not your own, it's God's (1 Corinthians 6:19). It also says to honor your mother and father (Exodus 20:12). So with that in mind, decide what is best for you and for your family.

Should Christians get their nipples, tongue, or belly button pierced?

If you want to experience tremendous amounts of pain, go for it. However, we would recommend taking out the nose ring anytime grandma comes to visit. She won't dig it. Trust us.

As far as your nipples and other private parts—unless you're going to do it yourself, or wait till you are married and have your spouse do it for you, we're not sure it's the best decision. We really can't imagine Jesus being real excited about some big sweaty guy giving you a "Prince Albert" or touching your other private parts just so you can have that piercing you've always wanted "down there."

Secondly, consider motive. Let's take the pierced belly button. What's the motive? Most would say, "It's fashionably cool." But the deeper issue is to draw attention to the midriff. A girl who pierces her belly button and puts a sparkly diamond there is screaming, "LOOK AT MY BODY! I AM AN OBJECT!" In return, a guy ganders at the midriff and then finds himself peeping in on the bare tummy. In most guys, thought builds upon thought and a fantasy develops. So it's not good for you or for others.

In our opinion, a godly female—

a. Was not designed to be an object,

b. Is not doing the right thing by leading guys' thoughts down the wrong path, and

c. Would not be so lacking in self-esteem that she needed to be admired in that way.

Having said all that, let me clarify. If someone you know already has piercings, don't judge them or assume you know their motive(s) for getting pierced. If you have piercings, don't judge yourself—even if it's a decision you now regret. And if you struggle with liking the feeling that guys are going gaga because of your pierced belly button, then ask God to redefine your self-image.

Chapter Nine

About XXXchurch

What's a Christian porn site, anyway?

What is the mission of your Web site and ministry?

Our official mission statement is: "XXXchurch exists to bring awareness, openness, accountability, and recovery to the church, society, and individuals in the issues of pornography and to begin to provide solutions through non-judgmental and creative means."

In a nutshell, that means we are seeking to make people aware of porn and to give help and hope to those who feel there is no way out. We want to encourage people to talk about porn and the issues related to it. We want Christians to be accountable for their actions and clean up their acts.

How are you guys able to surround yourselves with all of that stuff at porn shows without being tempted?

At first, we thought we wouldn't be able to handle it. How could *any* guy be surrounded by images of beautiful women and all these worldly things and not want a slice of it? But our experience has been very different from what we expected.

We have been to the "Red-Light District" in Amsterdam and to several porn shows. We have seen more images than anyone needs to see in a lifetime. But what we've realized is that this stuff is not fulfilling. These are not the happiest places on earth, and these girls are not amazing. The truth is this: It is all so temporary and shallow.

Jesus says he has come to give us life and a life more abundant (John 10:10). We truly have experienced a more abundant life; not because we get to see a bunch of porn at these shows, but because of the blessings and riches the Lord has granted to us. We look at the women who work in this industry with different eyes. Not with the eyes of the average consumer of porn, but with eyes that see through the make-up and the breast implants; eyes that see these women for who they are—very unhappy people. Many of them are lost and searching for something more than the affection of another man.

What about the people who work in the porn industry?

It is often refreshing to be around these people. They are so honest and open, and they don't put up any fronts. They tell you what they do, why they do it, and anything else you want to know. So many churchgoers like to pretend we have our act together. Some couples arrive smiling at church on Sunday morning, even though they fought the whole way there.

Jesus says his light will outshine any form of darkness. We feel honored and privileged to be God's witness to this industry. It saddens us to come in contact with these lost people, not only because they are not in a relationship with the Father, but also because most Christians don't care about them and will never do anything for them. That is why many of them have lost all interest in the church; that is why they have harsh things to say about religious folks; and that is why some of them may never know Jesus.

People, it is time to step out of our comfortable pews and get on the front lines! It is rewarding, it is amazing, and it is where Jesus would be.

What do your wives think about your ministry?

We'll let Craig's wife Jeanette tell you what she thinks: "I have been 100 percent behind this ministry from the beginning. I never worried that Craig would be pulled into sin or even temptation by being surrounded by porn things. Craig's desire is to serve God with his life and he has never swayed from that. When I first heard Mike and Craig wanted to create this ministry, I thought it was needed, but I didn't realize how much it was needed until after the site was launched. Once I got to see how porn ruins lives, I knew that God has truly called Craig to help people get through their issues. I fully trust that God will lead Craig away from any temptation."

103

Why do you call XXXchurch the "#1 Christian Porn Site"?

Our site is dedicated to porn and how it is affecting people. It's a porn site because that's what we're talking about. Nude pictures are so predictable and passé, don't you think? The truth is so much more interesting and satisfying. By the way, we are the number one Christian porn site because we are the only one! Besides, if we advertised ourselves as "The #1 Christian Site to Help You Deal with Your Addiction to Porn," who would visit our site or encourage someone else to check it out? And who would visit our site without feeling like they were the biggest pervert in the world?

We *are* the number one Christian porn site because it's in your face! It's larger than life! It's memorable. And it actually works! It's an amazing way to get people who would never intentionally look at a Christian Web page to come to our site.

Are you pro-porn?

It's unbelievable that we get this question so often. What do you think? OF COURSE WE ARE NOT PRO-PORN! Think, people! Let's put the pieces of the puzzle together. Pastors. Church. Accountability. The X3 pledge. Prayer wall. Does that sound like we are pro-porn? We do not judge, condemn, or point fingers at those who work in the porn industry or those who struggle with this issue, but we are not pro-porn.

There is no porn on our site because we think porn leaves you hanging. We are here to give you truth and inspiration, not nude pics. And Mike is not someone you want to see in the nude.

Why doesn't XXXchurch.com have more Scripture and overtly Christian stuff?

Well, we do have Bible studies and sermons you can listen to, as well as a prayer wall where you can post prayers. However, we refuse to allow our site to become the typical, cheesy Christian Web site with crosses and Bibles all over the place. (We also don't have corporate singing on the site, just in case you were looking for singing and clapping.) We don't want to communicate in Christian words and images that folks outside the church can't relate to. We just want to offer them the truth, communicated in a no-nonsense way.

What is your church affiliation or religion?

We are both ordained Christian pastors. Mike attends Crossroads Christian Church in Corona, California. Craig attends a new church plant in Lake Elsinore, California, called Tides Church. We attend with our wives and kids, and we help out in whatever way we can. We feel it is critical for us to be part of a local church and to be surrounded by a community of people who love us.

In addition to our involvement with these churches, we both work for Fireproof Ministries, the parent company to XXXchurch.com. Fireproof is a nondenominational parachurch ministry that exists to win people to the Lord and to train and develop people to meet the unmet needs of the world through culturally relevant ideas and programs.

105

Have you ever thought about doing a late-night TV commercial to compete with those phone-sex ads?

Why, yes, we have. In May 2003, we finished our first commercial: "Porn Stunts Your Growth." It aired on *The Man Show*, *The Howard Stern Show*, and *MTV*.

In February of 2004, we finished our second commercial called "For Pete's Sake." This commercial featured Pete the Porno Puppet and it was aimed at keeping kids away from pornography. It was filmed and directed by an actual pornographer of 15 years, and over 100 million people saw it. You can read more about this and our plans for other commercials at XXXchurch.com.

Chapter Ten

A Final Word

Now we've got a question for you...

So much of the book is about misdirected sexual activity: pornography, sexual addictions, masturbation, and premarital sex of every variety. That makes sense based on the nature of what we do in our ministry and work. We think it's very important to talk frankly about the very real consequences of extramarital sexual activity.

But this book is not intended to be a guide on what people should *not* do. We are seeking to offer a biblical vision for what teenagers *should* do. Of course, urging people to honor God's code of conduct for sexual purity brings "don'ts" to the table of conversation. We believe that is not all bad. Why? Because most young people embrace correction and efforts to build communication when the "don'ts" are explained with "whys."

109

Through all of our speakers, ministries, and outreach networks, we speak to over one million young people a year. These youth want someone to love them enough to help formulate healthy boundaries that will help them build healthy futures.

As we have answered teenagers' questions about sex via e-mail, we have discovered that the same questions are often repeated—over and over again. Yes, they are worded differently, and the details may vary, but the core issues remain the same. That realization fueled our desire to bring to the forefront those questions you could not ask your mama.

Throughout our ministry and this book, we have committed ourselves to three principles in answering teenagers' questions:

• Always be willing to answer what was asked and don't dodge the difficult.

• Always bring it back to the deeper spiritual issue with biblical truth.

• Always offer practical steps to gaining or keeping purity of motive, action, and mindset.

As you read and reread these questions and answers, we'd urge you to notice the very practical reasons to choose abstinence. Our answers offer a view of a more healthy and godly sexual perspective; we offer a bottom line of what God has in mind for young people—for all people—as they are maturing sexually, physically, and emotionally.

The end of our project is the beginning of your project. It's a challenging one—living a life that embraces purity while maintaining the positive vision of what God calls us to do. God's perfect plan was designed by his *all-knowing* ability to map out your best possible steps for life. So often his best is messed up because we follow what we think is best.

God does not want to take away your joy. He wants your joy to be complete and full. He doesn't want to take away from your future, only give to it. Call it "delayed gratification." The sacrifice you are willing to make today will bring a greater joy in the future. Your marriage, relationships, children, and mindset will all be infinitely stronger in the future if you choose to do what is right today.

I have never met nor heard of anyone who has said, "I lived a morally and sexually pure life and I regret it." Yet I *have* heard the opposite many times: "I have lived an impure life *and I regret it!*" Consider the value of your future and God's best. When you look deeply in that direction, you can be confident that God's love for you is more than capable of satisfying your deepest need for love.

Which brings us to one more question, and it is one we want to ask you:

Now that you've read all of these questions and answers, examined the biblical truths, heard the stories of pain and promise from other young people, and considered the practical steps to gaining or regaining a pure mindset and lifestyle—what are you going to do with the information?

Don't procrastinate with purity. Act today! It will mean the difference between wishing you had done the right thing and actually doing the right thing!

111

The Goofballs Speak

Mike Foster and Craig Gross are the founders of XXXchurch.com. These young pastors are forging the new frontier of ministry and as a result, they are delivering a dynamic message to churches and conferences across the United States. Their message is powerful and relevant to today's culture as they encourage individuals to live a life of outrageous Christianity. It's about taking a risk and connecting with the people whom the church classifies as unsafe and unpopular.

Mike and Craig have experienced shocking success over the last two years and have demonstrated what can happen when two goofballs decide to do something extreme. Their ministry has taken them to the darkest corners of society, which has allowed them to shine the light of Christ like never before. Both Christian and secular society are captivated by their story of being a light in the darkness. They have been featured on CNN, ABC News, NBC News and in the *Los Angeles Times, Playboy, New Man* magazine, *Outreach* magazine, *Sex TV, Decision Today, The 700 Club, Family News in Focus, Outdoor* magazine, *Charisma*, and *Penthouse*. They have also done numerous television and radio interviews for news agencies around the world.

Why the success? They have gone where most Christians won't go. They did something most would consider outrageous and completely revolutionary. They found that the greatest rewards are found not in church pews, but on the front lines. Their message will inspire and challenge you to take the next step in your faith and show you how you can be a light in the darkness too.

Let Mike and Craig share their incredible stories with your group and challenge them to truly understand what it means to be the salt of the earth and the light of the world.

Craig Gross

Craig Gross is a graduate of Hope International University with a B.A. in church ministry. He has worked in ministry for over nine years and has an incredible heart for saving the lost. He is twenty-eight years old and can relate to young people like no one else. Craig travels extensively across the United States, speaking at various churches, conferences, and conventions. In addition to co-founding X3church.com, he is the president of Fireproof Ministries, which touched the lives of over 200,000 people last year.

Mike Foster

Mike Foster is known for his irreverent and straight-talking approach as he helps churches across America build bridges to society. A native of Southern California, Mike has won the hearts of thousands by challenging the status quo and developing outrageous and controversial ideas. His passion for reaching the unsafe and unreachable people of our society has brought him to the front lines. As well as co-founding X3church.com, Mike is a pastor at one of the fastest-growing churches in North America.

The Goofballs' message is sure to:
• Inspire Christians to be outrageous in their faith!
• Motivate Christians to take the Gospel to individuals who are considered unsafe and unpopular.
• Educate the church about pornography and other issues facing modern-day culture and provide effective tools and solutions.
• Challenge people to live a life of integrity and have accountability, which will strengthen their effectiveness.

Mike and Craig are available for your next:
• Youth event
• Festival
• Men's breakfast or retreat
• Church service
• College chapel
• Custom XXXchurch event

To contact The Goofballs:
XXXchurch
P.O. Box 78268
Corona, CA 92877
949-862-5716
info@XXXchurch.com
www.thegoofballs.com or www.XXXchurch.com

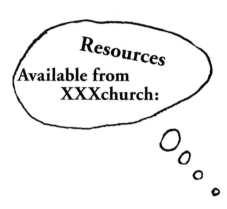

X3watch

X3watch is a FREE accountability program that helps with online integrity. It is offered at no charge by the ministry of XXXchurch. com and its supporters. Whenever you browse the Internet and access a site that may contain questionable material, the program will save the site name on your computer. Every two weeks or monthly (depending on your preference), a person of your choice (an accountability partner) will receive an e-mail containing all possible questionable sites you may have visited. This information is meant to encourage open and honest conversation between friends and help us all to be more accountable. This report goes only to your chosen accountability partners and is not stored or used by XXXchurch or any other organization.

121

X3 Help at Home Program

The X3 Help at Home Program is a ten-week, custom-designed program for men, teenagers, women, wives, and parents who are struggling with some type of sexual sin. In the first two years of XXXchurch, we have had over 10,000 emails and talked to thousands of people who need help. Often there is nowhere to turn—until now. The program is individually designed to meet you where you are and help you overcome your addiction in the privacy of your own home. The X3 Help at Home Program can help you!

Ask Mike and Craig

Now, we've never claimed to be the sharpest tools in the shed, but we want to try to help you discover the answers about God's will for your life. So if you have a question, email Mike and Craig at Questions@XXXchurch.com. Be forewarned, XXXchurch does not take any responsibility for what these two Goofballs might say. By the way, all questions we receive become the property of XXXchurch. We took the best questions we've received so far and put them in this book. Maybe your question will show up in the next one!

SEX

HAS A PRICE TAG

...XUALITY, SPIRITUALITY, AND SELF RESPECT — DISCUSSIONS ABOUT

...Stenzel
...rystal Kirgiss

IT'S NATURAL TO THINK ABOUT SEX,
BUT NO ONE WANTS TO TALK ABOUT IT.

SEX HAS A PRICE TAG GIVES YOU THE
STRAIGHT FACTS INCLUDING REAL
TESTIMONIES, ENCOURAGEMENT,
AND ADVISE ON EVERYTHING FROM
THE CONSEQUENCES OF SEX TO
ADVICE ON WHERE TO GO FOR HELP
TO HOW TO TALK TO FRIENDS AND
PARENTS ABOUT IT.

invert

RETAIL $9.99
ISBN 0310249716

www.youthspecialties.com/store

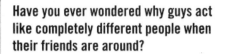